Ocean Animals

Sharks

by Christina Leaf

BLASTOFF!
Beginners

BELLWETHER MEDIA
MINNEAPOLIS, MN

Blastoff! Beginners are developed by literacy experts and educators to meet the needs of early readers. These engaging informational texts support young children as they begin reading about their world. Through simple language and high frequency words paired with crisp, colorful photos, Blastoff! Beginners launch young readers into the universe of independent reading.

Blastoff! Universe

Reading Level — Grade K

Grades 1-3

Grade 4

Sight Words in This Book 🔍

a	for	in	may	this
are	go	is	on	to
big	has	it	the	too
can	have	make	there	use
eat	help	many	they	who

This edition first published in 2021 by Bellwether Media, Inc.

No part of this publication may be reproduced in whole or in part without written permission of the publisher. For information regarding permission, write to Bellwether Media, Inc., Attention: Permissions Department, 6012 Blue Circle Drive, Minnetonka, MN 55343.

Library of Congress Cataloging-in-Publication Data

Names: Leaf, Christina, author.
Title: Sharks / by Christina Leaf.
Description: Minneapolis, MN : Bellwether Media, Inc., 2021. | Series: Ocean animals | Includes bibliographical references and index. |Audience: Grades PreK-2
Identifiers: LCCN 2020007742 (print) | LCCN 2020007743 (ebook) | ISBN 9781644873281 (library binding) | ISBN 9781681038155 (paperback) | ISBN 9781681037912 (ebook)
Subjects: LCSH: Sharks--Juvenile literature.
Classification: LCC QL638.9 L395 2021 (print) | LCC QL638.9 (ebook) | DDC 597.3--dc23
LC record available at https://lccn.loc.gov/2020007742
LC ebook record available at https://lccn.loc.gov/2020007743

Text copyright © 2021 by Bellwether Media, Inc. BLASTOFF! BEGINNERS and associated logos are trademarks and/or registered trademarks of Bellwether Media, Inc.

Editor: Amy McDonald   Designer: Andrea Schneider

Printed in the United States of America, North Mankato, MN.

Table of Contents

Sharks!

Who has those
big teeth?
It is a shark!

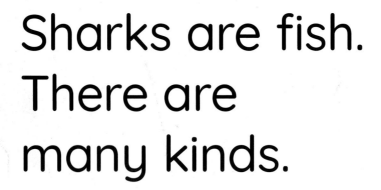

Sharks are fish.
There are
many kinds.

great white

hammerhead

blue

7

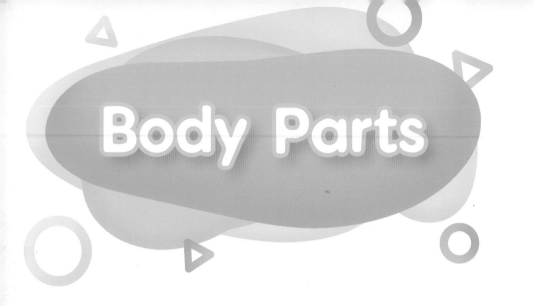

Body Parts

Sharks have **fins**.
Tail fins make
sharks go.

tail fin

Side fins help
sharks turn.

side fins

This is the
dorsal fin.
It is on the
shark's back.

dorsal fin

Sharks have **gills**.
They take in
water to breathe.

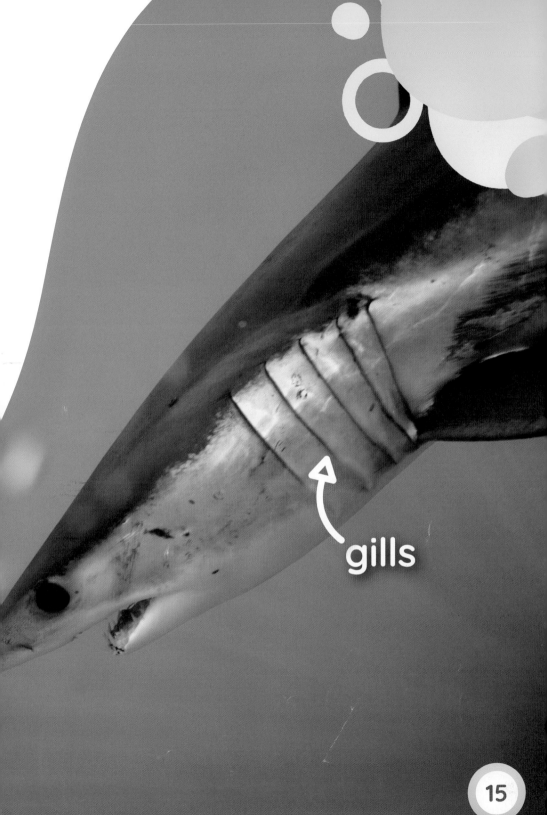

gills

On the Hunt

Sharks hunt
for food.
They eat fish.

Big sharks
may hunt seals.
They can eat
turtles, too.

seal

Most sharks bite food. They use sharp teeth. Chomp!

Shark Facts

Shark Body Parts

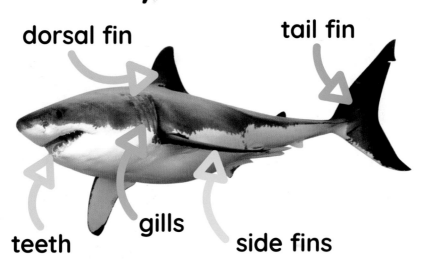

dorsal fin

tail fin

teeth

gills

side fins

Shark Food

fish

seals

turtles

Glossary

dorsal fin

a flat body part on the back of a shark

fins

flat body parts that stick out

gills

body parts that help fish breathe

To Learn More

ON THE WEB

FACTSURFER

Factsurfer.com gives you a safe, fun way to find more information.

1. Go to www.factsurfer.com.

2. Enter "sharks" into the search box and click 🔍.

3. Select your book cover to see a list of related content.

Index